American Moments

ABDO
Daughters

THE JAMESTOWN COLONY

By Alan Pierce

VISIT US AT
WWW.ABDOPUB.COM

Published by ABDO Publishing Company, 4940 Viking Drive, Edina, Minnesota 55435. Copyright © 2005 by Abdo Consulting Group, Inc. International copyrights reserved in all countries. No part of this book may be reproduced in any form without written permission from the publisher. ABDO & Daughters™ is a trademark and logo of ABDO Publishing Company.

Printed in the United States.

Edited by: Melanie A. Howard
Interior Production and Design: Terry Dunham Incorporated
Cover Design: Mighty Media
Photos: Corbis, North Wind Pictures

Library of Congress Cataloging-in-Publication Data

Pierce, Alan, 1966-
     Jamestown colony / Alan Pierce.
          p. cm. -- (American moments)
     Includes index.
     ISBN 1-59197-733-9
       1. Jamestown (Va.)--History--Juvenile literature. I. Title. II. Series.

     F234.J3P54 2004
     975.5'562--dc22

                                                                    2004050166

CONTENTS

JAMESTOWN

In May 1607, more than 100 Englishmen sailed to a land recently named Virginia. They had come to establish a colony in North America. A military officer named George Piercy accompanied the band of colonists. He reported an ominous beginning for the colony. Their first night ashore, the English came under attack from a local tribe. The English fired their guns and the attackers retreated into the forest.

The clash indicated that settling Virginia would be a formidable task. Indeed, founding the colony proved to be a difficult undertaking. Warfare with the local tribes was one problem. Soon, disease and starvation would claim many lives. The English had set up colonies in North America before, and they had all failed. This new settlement, called Jamestown, looked like it would join the list of abandoned colonies.

But Jamestown did not quickly disappear as other colonies had. It prevailed against many obstacles to become the first permanent English colony in North America. As such, Jamestown gave the English a foothold in the continent. This colony preceded more successful English colonies. The creation of these colonies changed the history of North America. Eventually, these colonies formed the basis of the United States.

THE *SUSAN CONSTANT*, THE *GODSPEED*, AND THE *DISCOVERY*

The ships pictured above are the Susan Constant, the Godspeed, and the Discovery. These were the ships that brought the English colonists to settle Jamestown. No one is certain what became of the three ships, but some information is known.

Experts believe that the larger ship Susan Constant, and the Godspeed, were used to shuttle coal when they returned to England. The Discovery belonged to the colonists, and stayed at Jamestown. It was used for trade and to explore the eastern coast, including Cape Cod. Charts made from these explorations may have aided the Pilgrims when they set up a colony in 1620.

SPAIN AND ENGLAND

England was not the first European country to establish a colony in North America. Many years before Jamestown, Spain had founded settlements on the continent. In 1492, Christopher Columbus sailed from Spain to islands in the Caribbean Sea. He had hoped to find a shorter trade route to Asia. Instead, Columbus had reached a continent unknown to Europeans.

Spain soon colonized the islands in the Caribbean Sea. From this base, Spain began its conquest of Central America. In 1519,

Christopher Columbus

Hernán Cortés led a force of Spaniards against the Aztec Empire in present-day Mexico. By 1521, the Spanish had defeated the Aztecs. Another Spaniard named Francisco Pizarro fought a campaign against the Incan Empire in South America. Between 1531 and 1532, the Spanish conquered this wealthy empire.

The conquests in Central and South America brought an immense fortune to Spain. These regions in the Americas possessed enormous mineral resources. Over the years, these colonies transported tons of gold and silver to Spain, making that country very rich and powerful.

Other countries in Europe feared Spain's might and began attacking Spanish treasure ships. The rivalry between Spain and England was especially strong. One reason for this hostility was religion. Spain's King Philip II championed Catholicism, and England had discarded Catholicism for Protestantism. Each country saw the other as a threat to its religion.

In order to compete with Spain, England began to try to set up its own colonies in North America. Sir Humphrey

Sir Humphrey Gilbert

Gilbert organized one of England's first attempts. In August 1583, his expedition of 260 men reached what is now Newfoundland in Canada.

Gilbert's men, however, were not the first Europeans to reach this area. More than 30 fishing boats from France, Portugal, Spain, and England were already there. Nevertheless, Gilbert claimed this region for England and established a colony.

The colony quickly fell apart. Many of the men were unhappy, and the expedition lost its largest ship. Gilbert decided to return to England. But his ship disappeared while sailing back. England's first attempt to start a North American colony had ended in failure.

ROANOKE

The next Englishman to attempt to colonize North America was Sir Walter Raleigh. He was Sir Humphrey Gilbert's half brother. After Gilbert's death, England's Queen Elizabeth I gave Raleigh authority to set up colonies in North America. In 1584, Raleigh arranged for two ships to explore the North American coast. The expedition scouted the coast of what is now North Carolina. In addition, the explorers brought back two indigenous people named Manteo and Wanchese. The English hoped to use these two men as interpreters on other expeditions.

After the voyage, the English named the new land they had explored. They called it Virginia in honor of Elizabeth I, who was not married and was known as the Virgin Queen. Virginia, however, represented a much larger area than it does today. The area stretched along what is today much of the United States's eastern coast.

In 1585, Raleigh sent a second expedition to North America. By June, this expedition arrived at

Sir Walter Raleigh

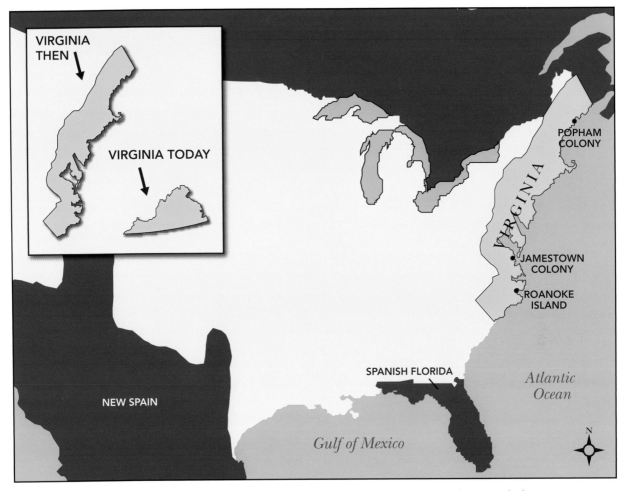

In the sixteenth and early seventeenth centuries, the English referred to much of the North American east coast as Virginia.

Roanoke Island off the coast of present-day North Carolina. The English built a fort on the island and left behind 107 men. Among those who traveled to Roanoke Island was an artist named John White. He made many drawings of indigenous people, plants, and animals living in the Roanoke area.

In June 1586, the English pirate Sir Francis Drake visited Roanoke Island. Rather than stay on the island, the colonists accepted Drake's offer to return to England. Two ships later arrived to find the colony abandoned. Some men from these ships stayed behind at the Roanoke fort.

A map of Roanoke Island and surrounding areas

Raleigh attempted to establish another colony in 1587. This effort to colonize North America was different from other English attempts. The expedition was not restricted to men. Seventeen women and nine boys accompanied the group of settlers. The colonists also brought Manteo, who could communicate with the indigenous people. In the spring, Manteo and the English sailed west in the *Lion* and two smaller vessels.

The colonists' original plan was to establish a colony in the Chesapeake Bay area. However, the man piloting the expedition's ships left the colonists on Roanoke Island in July 1587. The artist John White had returned with the colonists, but this time he served as governor. White's colonists used the Roanoke fort built by the previous English settlers. But the men who had stayed to protect the fort had disappeared.

In August 1587, Governor White prepared to return to England to acquire more supplies. Before he left, he made an agreement with the colonists. If they moved, the colonists should indicate their new place by carving the location into a tree. A cross added to the carving meant the colonists had left the settlement while being attacked.

White arrived in England in November 1587. Unfortunately, war between Spain and England delayed his return to Virginia. Spain had assembled a tremendous fleet known as the Armada to defeat the English at sea. A Spanish army was then expected to invade England. Spain launched the Armada against England in the summer of 1588. The English fleet, in combination with stormy weather, damaged the Armada and ruined Spain's planned invasion.

In March 1590, White was allowed to return to Virginia. By August, he reached Roanoke. The colonists, however, were gone. At the settlement, White found the word *Croatoan* carved into a post at the stockade. There was a nearby island called Croatoan. In fact, Manteo was from this island. White intended to search for the colonists on Croatoan, but a storm prevented him from sailing there. He returned to England without finding the colonists.

The colonists were never located. Their fate remains a mystery. Consequently, Roanoke is often referred to as the "Lost Colony." Historians have offered some theories about what might have happened to the colonists. Some think the colonists joined indigenous people and were killed by the powerful Powhatan tribe. Others have speculated that the colonists survived with a friendly tribe.

THE VIRGINIA COMPANY

In 1604, England's new king, James I, made peace with Spain. This development benefited England's efforts to establish colonies in North America. The English no longer needed to worry as much about the Spanish attacking new colonies overseas.

The failure of England's earlier colonies showed that a huge investment was needed for a colony. The resources of a few people were not enough to make a colony succeed. One way to encourage trade was to form a joint-stock company. Many people could invest their money in this type of company. Consequently, the company's success or failure would not depend on one person.

Powerful and wealthy men in England were interested in forming a trading company. They requested a charter from James I to set up the venture. In April 1606, the king authorized a charter to form the Virginia Company of London. The company's purpose

King James I of England

12

was to establish colonies in the Virginia region along the North American east coast.

The Virginia Company was divided into two other companies. One was called the London Company and the other was called the Plymouth Company. The London Company was responsible for establishing colonies in the southern part of Virginia. The Plymouth Company had authority to found colonies in the northern part of Virginia.

The investors hoped that establishing colonies would make them a large profit. There were several ways the Virginia colonists could make money. For example, they were expected to look for gold and trade with the indigenous people. They could also search for a sea route to Asia. This would allow for more trade between Asia and Europe. Explorers had been looking for decades for a sea passage that linked the Atlantic and Pacific oceans.

Both companies planned colonies at about the same time. Thanks to earlier explorations, they knew where they wanted to start their settlements. The London Company chose to set up a colony in the Chesapeake Bay area. The Plymouth Company prepared to send colonists to present-day Maine.

In the summer of 1607, about 100 men from the Plymouth Company arrived in modern-day Maine. They set up a colony near the mouth of the Kennebec River. The men built Fort St. George and constructed several other buildings. In addition, the colonists started a fur trade with the Abenaki tribe and built a boat named the *Virginia*.

Many colonists left, however, after the harsh winter. The colony's fortunes suffered another blow when one of its leaders, George Popham,

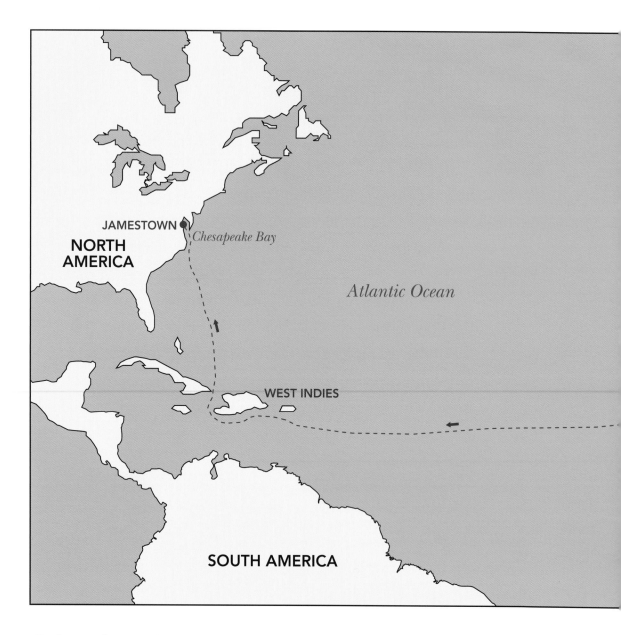

died in 1608. That year, the remaining colonists abandoned the settlement and returned to England. After the colony's failure, many investors in the Plymouth Company contributed their money to the London Company.

Meanwhile, the London Company had planned its Virginia colony. The Virginia Company chose John Smith to accompany the expedition to North America. Smith was a soldier who had already led a life of

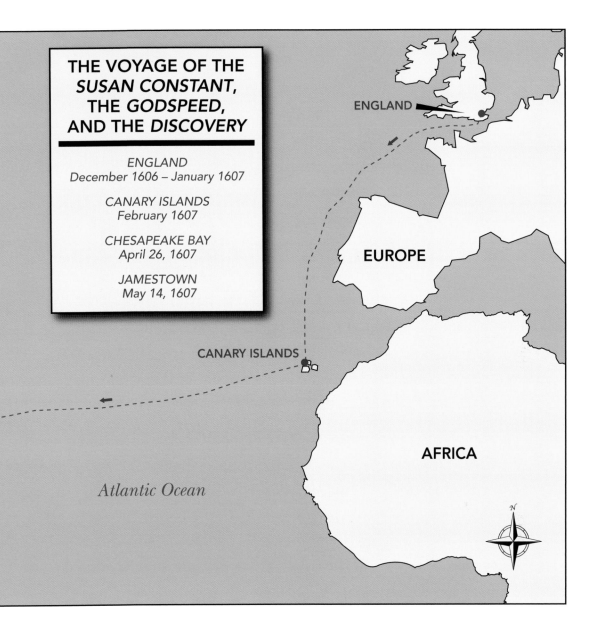

**THE VOYAGE OF THE
SUSAN CONSTANT,
THE *GODSPEED*,
AND THE *DISCOVERY***

ENGLAND
December 1606 – January 1607

CANARY ISLANDS
February 1607

CHESAPEAKE BAY
April 26, 1607

JAMESTOWN
May 14, 1607

ENGLAND

EUROPE

CANARY ISLANDS

AFRICA

Atlantic Ocean

adventure. He fought against the Turks in central Europe.
Eventually, he was captured and sold into slavery in Russia.
However, Smith escaped and made his way back to England in 1604.

In December 1606, the ships *Susan Constant*, *Godspeed*, and *Discovery*
sailed from England for North America. Captain Christopher
Newport commanded the small fleet of 140 men and 4 boys.
During the voyage, 39 people died.

Another difficulty during the voyage involved John Smith. He argued with other leaders of the expedition. These disagreements led to Smith being locked in shackles and accused of mutiny.

On April 26, 1607, the three ships reached Chesapeake Bay. That same day, colonists opened sealed instructions from the London Company. Much to the leaders' surprise, the instructions named Smith to the colony's seven-member council. The other leaders, however, voted Smith off the assembly.

Newport's ships sailed around Chesapeake Bay while the colonists searched for a good location for a settlement. The colonists finally sailed up a river. They named it the James River after the king. On May 14, 1607, the English landed on a peninsula about 30 miles (48.3 km) from the bay to establish a colony. They selected the site because it offered a good defensive position against attack. It also provided a deep harbor for larger ships.

The settlers managed to build some homes and a church, but they failed to plant a crop. Many of the colonists considered themselves to be gentlemen. At that time, a gentleman was someone who did not labor for a living. Only 24 of the colonists were laborers. They called the settlement James Cittie after King James I. Later, the settlement was called Jamestown.

The English needed to protect their colony against possible attacks from the Spanish and local tribes. To defend the settlement, they surrounded their buildings with a wooden fort. The fort made a triangle around the settlement. Each of the corners formed a circular watchtower. Within the walls of the fort, the colonists struggled in their new environment.

John Smith led the Jamestown Colony. He also made accurate maps of Virginia and wrote about his adventures in North America.

JOHN SMITH

The English colonists had a good reason to be wary of an attack from indigenous people. Jamestown existed near the powerful Powhatan Confederacy. The confederacy received its name from its founder, Chief Powhatan. He had banded together about 30 tribes to form this group. More than 12,000 people made up the confederacy. About 3,000 of the Powhatans were warriors.

The local tribes and the colonists fought almost as soon as the English arrived. However, the Powhatans and the colonists also traded. Early on, the residents of Jamestown depended on Powhatan corn for food. In return, the colonists traded glass and copper beads. Copper was especially valuable to the Powhatans. A tribe hostile to the Powhatans controlled the local source of copper.

The complicated relationship between the colonists and the Powhatans can be seen in John Smith's experience. Although Smith was no longer under arrest, the colony's leaders still disliked him. They dealt with Smith by sending him away to explore the region.

In December 1607, the Powhatans ambushed Smith and a small group who were exploring the Chickahominy River. The Englishmen with Smith were killed, but Smith was captured. He was now the prisoner of Opechancanough, who had led the ambush. Opechancanough was also Chief Powhatan's younger brother.

Englishmen trade hats, knives, and other items with indigenous people.

He brought Smith to the important Powhatan village of Werowocomoco, north of Jamestown.

Smith was brought before Chief Powhatan. The Powhatans acted as if they were about to execute Smith. But as they did so, Chief Powhatan's young daughter named Matoaka threw herself over Smith. He was not executed, and returned to Jamestown. Smith believed that Matoaka had saved his life out of her love for the English. Matoaka later became known to the English by the name Pocahontas.

The account of Pocahontas's rescue of John Smith is one of the most famous stories in colonial history. It is also controversial because historians do not agree on what the event meant. Many historians doubt that Chief Powhatan intended to kill Smith. Instead, they think the event was a ceremony to make Smith a minor chief. Others disagree and accept Smith's version of his rescue.

John Smith had survived his encounter with the Powhatans. The colonists, however, were in trouble. Many of their troubles stemmed from the James River. The river provided the colonists with their drinking water, but the water quality was poor. Germs that caused diseases, such as typhus and dysentery, thrived in the swampy water.

The James River was also a potential source of salt poisoning. This hazard arose because tides from the ocean carried saltwater up the river. Salt poisoning was more likely during summer when the river's water level was low. Under this condition, saltwater contaminated the river. The local tribes knew the peninsula was an unhealthy site and had moved away long ago.

Disease and malnutrition claimed the lives of many colonists. In January 1608, only 38 of the colonists were still alive. At this time, Captain Newport arrived with supplies and 120 new settlers. Unluckily for the colonists, a fire destroyed most of the supplies. The fire also burned down many of the buildings in Jamestown. That winter, the colonists lived mostly in three buildings.

The situation at Jamestown continued to worsen during the next several months. Smith left Jamestown to explore and to make a map of Chesapeake Bay. Meanwhile, the colonists had become obsessed with finding gold. They believed that gold existed in a mineral they

POCAHONTAS AND JOHN SMITH

Pocahontas, or Matoaka, has been romantically linked with Captain John Smith in many plays, books, and poems. In 1995, Walt Disney Pictures even made an animated film called Pocahontas in which John Smith and Pocahontas fall in love.

Several sources, including the Powhatan Nation, contend that the legend of the romance between Smith and Pocahontas is pure fiction. Many scholars point out that Smith himself estimated that Pocahontas was only 10 years old. Other estimates only placed her age as high as 14. Smith himself was 28 at the founding of Jamestown.

Others have argued that if Pocahontas were even just 12 years old, she would have been considered old enough to marry by her own tribe.

Supporters of the Smith and Pocahontas romance also refer to the fact that the Council of Jamestown accused Smith of wanting to marry Pocahontas to become "king" of Virginia.

The debate about whether or not John Smith and Pocahontas ever had a romantic relationship has never been settled. But it has captured the imaginations of many, and has survived for more than 400 years.

A portrait of Pocahontas

found called mica. At one point, the colonists sent a ship loaded with mica back to England. The mica, however, was worthless.

While the colonists searched for gold, they neglected important duties. They had not planted crops or cleared land. But they were fortunate. Smith returned from his explorations with food he had acquired from the indigenous people. On September 10, 1608, Smith became president of the colony.

As the new president, Smith carried out major changes in Jamestown. He imposed rigid discipline on the men. They were required to work several hours each day. Smith also initiated another serious policy. He declared that colonists who would not work would starve.

Smith's leadership made him unpopular with the settlers, but his presidency also benefited the colony. The colonists built 20 houses so that everyone at Jamestown had a suitable home. They also dug a well, which provided them with an alternative to the James River for drinking water. In addition, the colonists planted crops, improved their fort, and began producing tar, pitch, and soap.

Jamestown was further strengthened in the fall of 1608. Captain Newport brought 70 new colonists to Jamestown. Among these colonists were the first two women to arrive at Jamestown. One woman, Mistress Forrest, was already married. Her maid, Anne Burras, soon married colonist John Laydon. The ceremony was the first marriage in the colony.

The worth of Smith's leadership was demonstrated during the winter of 1608-1609. Not many colonists died at Jamestown during

Colonists hard at work creating the Jamestown Colony

this time. However, Smith's command of the colony was coming to
an end. In May 1609, the Virginia Company approved a new charter
for the colony. This charter named a governor to replace the colony's
president and council. Thomas West, Baron De La Warre, was
appointed to serve as Jamestown's first governor.

Smith was still president of the colony when he suffered a serious
accident. In September 1609, a spark ignited a fire on Smith's
gunpowder bag. He jumped into a river to put out the flames, but
he sustained painful injuries. After the accident, Smith decided to
return to England.

SURVIVAL

John Smith's departure led to a collapse of leadership at Jamestown. De La Warre had not arrived yet, and leaders at the colony feuded with one another. In the meantime, the colonists ate up their food supplies and quit fishing.

Jamestown faced other problems as well. The Powhatans began attacking the colonists and killing livestock. Faced with this violence, the colonists withdrew behind the walls of their fort.

Trapped inside their fort without food, hunger made the colonists desperate. They were reduced to eating horses, rats, dogs, and snakes. Some colonists even used the starch intended for their clothes to make porridge. Colonists who turned to the indigenous people for help were killed. There were also cases of cannibalism.

The colonists referred to this grim winter as the "starving time." Disease and malnutrition took a staggering toll on the English residents at Jamestown. In October 1609, about 500 people had lived in Jamestown. By May 1610, their numbers had dropped to 60. The colony had lost about 80 percent of its population within a few months.

At this time, Deputy Governor Sir Thomas Gates arrived at the colony with two ships. The colony's situation was so dire that he decided to take the colonists back to England. They boarded his ship and sailed down the James River.

DID YOU KNOW?

Did you know that Thomas West, Baron De La Warre and other Englishmen had earlier experiences with colonization? The English colonized Ireland before they set up colonies in North America.

Sir Walter Raleigh, Sir Humphrey Gilbert, and De La Warre had all helped suppress uprisings in Ireland.

For centuries, England had controlled areas of Ireland. But in the sixteenth century, England greatly expanded its control of the island. The English seized Irish territory and turned this land into plantations for Protestants from England and Scotland.

This map of Ireland was made in 1596. The right side of the map is north.

The Irish were mostly Catholic. They resented being ruled by English Protestants. During the reign of Queen Elizabeth I, the English had put down three major Irish rebellions. The English believed that they were bringing a superior culture to Ireland. They saw the Irish as ungrateful barbarians for resisting conversion to a superior English civilization. Later, the English regarded indigenous people in Virginia the same way.

Gates's ships had only traveled about 14 miles (23 km) when they encountered three other vessels. These other ships brought Governor De La Warre, supplies, and 150 new colonists. Reinforced with more settlers and additional supplies, the English headed back to the colony they had recently abandoned.

De La Warre and other governors brought back strong leadership that had been missing since John Smith left Jamestown. The English began to restore Jamestown by repairing homes and cleaning up the settlement. They also expanded their activity beyond Jamestown. At the mouth of the James River, the colonists built two forts.

After De La Warre left the colony in March 1611, Gates served as acting governor. Deputy Governor Sir Thomas Dale also held considerable power. In September, Dale led a group of men up the James River. They established a new settlement called Henrico, also called Henricus.

Together, Gates and Dale brought back a military style of discipline to the colony. In 1612, they established a written legal code. These laws were called the *Lawes and Orders Divine, Politique, and Martial for the Colony of Virginia*. The code was extremely harsh. Anyone who attempted to leave the colony would be put to death. Stealing also carried the death penalty. Those who showed up late for work more than once were whipped. Although these laws were severe, they prevented the colony from falling apart.

Thomas West, Baron De La Warre arrives in Jamestown, Virginia.

JOHN ROLFE AND POCAHONTAS

The Virginia Colony had been established to make money. But in its first few years the colony had barely survived. The colonists had managed to ship some products and raw materials back to England. These items, such as glass, pitch, tar, and iron, failed to earn money for the Virginia Company.

To increase profits, the colonists considered tobacco as a crop they could trade with England. The indigenous people grew and smoked tobacco, and the plant was a valuable commodity for the Spanish.

Tobacco raised in Virginia, however, had a disadvantage. For those who liked tobacco, the Virginia plant tasted bitter. Spanish tobacco was considered better. The Virginia colonists later managed to acquire tobacco seeds from the West Indies. By 1612, colonist John Rolfe was successfully growing tobacco with seeds from the West Indies and South America.

Tobacco turned out to be a boon for the Virginia colonists. The plant flourished in Virginia's long, hot growing season. It also became highly profitable as exports of tobacco increased. A farmer raising tobacco in Virginia could possibly earn more in one year than a farmer in England could make in ten years.

Raising tobacco created more demand for labor. Much of this work was supplied by white indentured servants. These types of

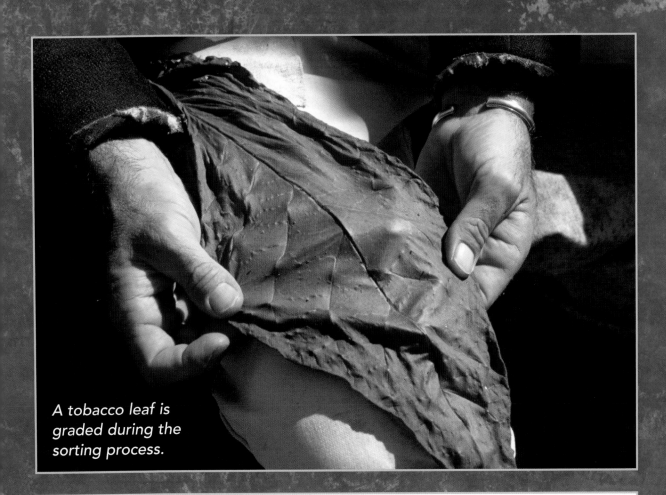

A tobacco leaf is graded during the sorting process.

THE EARLY DAYS OF TOBACCO

Tobacco was cultivated for many years by the indigenous peoples of North and South America. The plant first entered English society in 1586. It was brought back by colonists from the New World who were seen smoking it in a pipe. Within the next 20 years, tobacco smoking and chewing became more common in England.

But by the early 1600s, concerns about health risks to smokers sparked some debate. A publication written in 1602 by an anonymous author denounced tobacco. It compared the smoke from tobacco to the soot that caused illnesses in chimney sweeps.

King James I published his own pamphlet condemning tobacco. He called smoking "a custom loathsome to the eye, hateful to the nose, harmful to the brain, [and] dangerous to the lungs." The king did not, however, ban tobacco. Instead, he put a tax on tobacco imports, which raised a great deal of money.

Tobacco was soon found to be addictive. Serious health concerns about tobacco use such as increased risk of emphysema, heart attack, and stroke were discovered over the next 400 years. Today, most people consider smoking a dangerous habit.

workers agreed to work for four to seven years in return for transportation to Virginia. Ship captains delivered indentured servants to Virginia where people needing workers bought the servants' labor contracts. After their term was finished, indentured servants received some money and, in some cases, land.

The popularity of cultivating tobacco also increased the colonists' desire for land. As they expanded their tobacco fields, the colonists advanced into Powhatan territory. These intrusions increased the tension between the English and the Powhatans.

In 1613, the English sailor Sir Samuel Argall was traveling up the Potomac River when he learned that Pocahontas was nearby. He saw this as a good opportunity to give the English an advantage over the Powhatans. Argall captured Pocahontas and brought her back to Jamestown. The English then made Chief Powhatan an offer. They wanted to exchange his daughter for seven English prisoners being held by the Powhatans.

As the English and Chief Powhatan argued, Pocahontas underwent a major change. She converted to Christianity and was baptized. Her new name was Rebecca. Moreover, John Rolfe wanted to marry her. Sir Thomas Dale was now the colony's governor, and he approved of the marriage. Chief Powhatan also agreed. Both the governor and the chief hoped the marriage might bring peace to the colonists and the Powhatans.

In April 1614, Pocahontas and John Rolfe were married. The marriage did achieve peace in the colony, which the English referred to as the "Peace of Pocahontas." But Pocahontas and Rolfe did not remain in Virginia during this time of peace. In 1616, they traveled to England to encourage colonization of Virginia.

This is one artist's depiction of the baptism of Pocahontas.

In England, Pocahontas was respected as a chief's daughter. She attended King James I's royal court, and the bishop of London treated her as an honored guest. At one point, John Smith visited her.

While Pocahontas and Rolfe prepared to sail back to Virginia, Pocahontas fell ill and died in 1617. Some historians think she may have died of smallpox. Others believe that tuberculosis or pneumonia caused her death. John Rolfe and Pocahontas's young son, Thomas, was also sick. Rather than take the boy across the ocean, Rolfe decided to leave him in England. Rolfe's brother raised Thomas while Rolfe returned to Virginia.

MORE LIBERTY AND NO LIBERTY

Pocahontas had helped bring attention to Jamestown. And tobacco was becoming an important crop, but the amount of exports remained small for a time. There were still no profits for the Virginia Company's stockholders to share. This made them unhappy with the colony. A new approach was needed.

The Virginia Company adopted a new charter that brought changes to the colony. It became known as the Great Charter. The charter included reforms designed to make the colony more attractive to potential settlers.

One significant development was the creation of a legislative body that would give the colonists more power. This body was called the House of Burgesses. The governor, council, and elected representatives called burgesses made up the assembly. Any act passed by the assembly could be vetoed by the governor. Also, acts approved by the House of Burgesses did not become lawful until authorized by the Virginia Company.

Virginia's new governor, Sir George Yeardley, presented the charter when he arrived at the colony in 1619. On July 30, the House of Burgesses met for its first session. This date marked the first time that a legislative assembly had met in an English colony in North America. The session continued for six days at a church in Jamestown. During

Excavated foundation of the statehouse at Jamestown

this time, the assembly made decisions about relations with the indigenous people. The House of Burgesses also established taxes for the colony.

Politics was not the only aspect that the Great Charter had changed. The charter also made it easier for colonists to acquire land. Colonists who were not indentured servants received 100 acres (40.5 ha) of land. They were also given more land if they owned shares in the company. Indentured servants were promised 100 acres (40.5 ha) after they finished their service. New settlers secured 50 acres (20.2 ha) of land when they arrived in Virginia.

The new policy spurred more colonists to settle in Virginia. In 1619, about 1,200 settlers moved to Virginia. These settlers included shipbuilders from France, sawyers from Germany, and glassmakers from Italy. Within the next couple of years, thousands of colonists arrived.

The Great Charter had expanded opportunities for colonists. But another event showed the limitations of freedom in the colony. In August 1619, a Dutch ship brought about 20 people of African descent to Jamestown. Governor Yeardley and a colonist named Abraham Piersey bought the Africans. Most historians assume that these Africans were treated as indentured servants. Slavery as an institution did not form in Virginia until the 1660s.

As indentured servants, Africans could own property after their service was completed. Some did so. However, African indentured servants experienced unfair treatment. For example, they often served longer than white servants did.

Virginia still faced dangers. One threat that remained was the Powhatans. The colonists and the Powhatans had experienced a few years of peace after Pocahontas's marriage. But Chief Powhatan had died in 1618, and his brother, Opechancanough, had become chief. Opechancanough distrusted the colonists. He planned an attack against the English settlers who had been pushing onto Powhatan land.

On March 22, 1622, the Powhatans unleashed a surprise attack on the colonists. Opechancanough's warriors killed 347 men, women, and children throughout the colony.

The attack was devastating for the colonists. But the massacre also ruined the Virginia Company. The company had already been in poor financial shape, and the attack hurt the company even more. In 1624, King James I ended the company and took control of Virginia. Virginia then became a royal colony.

The House of Burgesses survived the change in the colony's status. James I had not discussed the future of the assembly when he assumed power over the colony. Nevertheless, the colony's first royal governor,

Virginia colonists warring with a local tribe

Francis Wyatt, summoned the House of Burgesses for a meeting in 1625. Afterward, the assembly continued to meet to pass laws.

The fact that Virginia had become a crown colony did not alter the hostility between the colonists and the Powhatans. In April 1644, Opechancanough led another attack against the colonists. More than 400 settlers were killed in this attack. The English responded by destroying the villages of the Powhatans. In 1646, Governor William Berkeley commanded a force that captured Opechancanough. A guard killed Opechancanough while the chief was being held in a prison in Jamestown.

After Opechancanough's death, the Powhatan tribes agreed in a treaty to give up land to the English. The colonists promised not to settle west of this land. But the colonists broke the agreement and continued to expand west.

BACON'S REBELLION

Conflict with surrounding tribes later contributed to a rebellion in Virginia. Strife between settlers and a tribe called the Susquehannock had been growing. Governor William Berkeley built forts on the Virginia frontier to protect the settlers. But this strategy failed to satisfy settlers on the frontier. They wanted to attack the local tribes.

Governor Berkeley was unpopular for other reasons as well.

Nathaniel Bacon

He had suspended elections for choosing members of the House of Burgesses. The assembly still met, but people could not elect new burgesses. Furthermore, the House of Burgesses imposed heavy taxes on the colonists.

In April 1676, a colonist named Nathaniel Bacon led an attack against local tribes. Bacon was no ordinary colonist. He was the son of an English lord, and related to Berkeley by marriage. In fact, Bacon served on the governor's council.

Jamestown, Virginia, is in flames during Bacon's Rebellion.

Bacon's attack created a split between Berkeley and himself. Berkeley had not ordered the attack. The governor announced that Bacon was a rebel. Later, Berkeley pardoned Bacon and gave him the authority to fight the local tribes. For unknown reasons, the governor again declared Bacon to be a rebel.

Bacon's followers took control of Jamestown but eventually left the city to fight indigenous tribes. In September 1676, Bacon's supporters returned to Jamestown, forcing Governor Berkeley to leave the city. They also raided the properties of rich landowners and burned down Jamestown.

Soon after, the rebellion lost its momentum. In October, Bacon died, possibly from dysentery. Governor Berkeley regained control of the colony and hanged more than 20 of Bacon's supporters.

The calamity of Bacon's Rebellion cost Jamestown its place of importance in Virginia. Rebuilding was slow after the fire. The House of Burgesses convened at other locations. One location was called Middle Plantation. Eventually, the colonists built a new statehouse in Jamestown. However, it burned down in 1698. The next year, Virginia moved its capital to Middle Plantation, which was renamed Williamsburg.

After losing its status as the capital city, Jamestown began to decline. Within 50 years, the city had practically disappeared and the site had become farmland. Later, a brick church tower marked the only visible trace of the colony's existence.

Opposite page: *Nathaniel Bacon confronts Governor William Berkeley.*

REDISCOVERY

In the late nineteenth century, interest in Jamestown revived. The Society for the Preservation of Virginia Antiquities supported work to find the colony's fort. Since then, archaeologists have excavated the fort and other buildings at Jamestown. Thousands of artifacts have been discovered at the site. These objects include armor, tools, ceramics, and coins.

Today, Jamestown is part of the Colonial National Historic Park. In addition to Jamestown, the park also includes Cape Henry. This is where the English colonists first landed. Visitors can see Governor Berkeley's plantation home. They can also visit the excavation sites of the fort and statehouse.

Near the original site is the Jamestown Settlement. This is a museum where people can learn more about the lives of the colonists and the Powhatans. It features a Powhatan village, a colonial fort, and a dock with replicas of the *Susan Constant*, *Godspeed*, and *Discovery*. People dressed in historically accurate costumes demonstrate how the settlers and the Powhatans lived in the seventeenth century.

But Jamestown is more than a museum and place to discover artifacts. The colony helped shape the direction that the English colonies and the United States would take. Jamestown's House of

The Jamestown Settlement allows tourists to see colonial living.

Burgesses gave rise to the form of government that prevails in the United States today. The colony's buildings are mostly gone. But the idea of representative government that was carried out in Jamestown remains alive.

TIMELINE

1585 In June, Sir Walter Raleigh makes the first attempt to establish a colony on Roanoke Island.

1587 In July, colonists set up another colony on Roanoke Island. Governor John White leaves the colony in August.

1590 White returns to Roanoke Island in August. He discovers that the colony has been abandoned, and finds the word *Croatoan* carved into a post.

1606 In April, King James I authorizes a charter to form the Virginia Company.

1607 On May 14, the Virginia Company's colonists found Jamestown.

In the summer, about 100 men found a colony at Fort St. George at the mouth of the Kennebec River in present-day Maine. Many colonists return to England after a harsh winter.

In December, members of the Powhatan Confederacy capture, John Smith. He credits Pocahontas with saving his life.

1608 On September 10, John Smith becomes president of the Jamestown Colony.

1609 to 1610
During the winter, the colonists suffer what they call the "starving time."

 1619
Governor George Yeardley presents the Great Charter to the colonists at Jamestown.

On July 30, the first legislative assembly in North America meets for six days at a church in Jamestown.

In August, the first Africans are brought to Jamestown and sold into service.

 1622
On March 22, the Powhatan tribe attacks the Jamestown settlers.

1624
King James I takes control of Virginia and makes it a royal colony.

1644
In April, Chief Opechancanough leads another attack against the Jamestown colonists.

1646
Chief Opechancanough is captured and killed.

1676
A colonist named Nathaniel Bacon starts Bacon's Rebellion. Bacon and his supporters burn down much of Jamestown.

 1699
The capital of Virginia is moved to Middle Plantation, which is renamed Williamsburg.

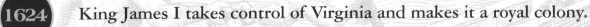

American Moments

FAST FACTS

On August 18, 1587, an important event occurred at the Roanoke Colony. Governor John White's daughter, Ellinor Dare, gave birth to the first English child born in North America. The girl was named Virginia after the colony.

The Jamestown colonists knew of the Lost Colony of Roanoke. They made several attempts to find the Roanoke colonists. When Native Americans reported seeing European settlements, Jamestown colonists investigated. However, the lost settlers were never found.

Ambassador Pedro de Zuniga, possibly a Spanish spy, made the only known sketch of James Fort in about 1609. He drew it on a tracing of a 1608 map of Virginia by John Smith. Zuniga later sent this rough drawing to King Philip III of Spain.

Women sent to Jamestown in 1620 and 1621 were known as tobacco brides. A man who married a tobacco bride paid 120 pounds (54 kg) of tobacco for her. This payment covered the cost of her voyage across the Atlantic Ocean.

Archaeological evidence suggests that Jamestown settlers found many ways to entertain themselves. Pieces of musical instruments, games, and toys have been unearthed at the site. These artifacts include dice made from bone, and a figure of a little boy made from lead.

WEB SITES
WWW.ABDOPUB.COM

Would you like to learn more about the Jamestown Colony? Please visit **www.abdopub.com** to find up-to-date Web site links about the Jamestown Colony and other American moments. These links are routinely monitored and updated to provide the most current information available.

A woman reenacts colonial work at the Jamestown Settlement.

GLOSSARY

archaeologist: one who studies the remains of people and activities from ancient times.

artifact: anything made by human skill or work a long time ago.

burgess: a representative in colonial government.

Catholic: a Christian who belongs to the Catholic Church, specifically the Roman Catholic Church.

charter: a written contract that states a colony's boundaries and form of government.

confederacy: a group of people joined together in an alliance.

convene: to meet or assemble.

dysentery: a disease that causes severe diarrhea.

excavate: to dig up or expose buried ruins/fossils/settlements.

indenture: a contract that binds a person to work for another person for a stated time period.

indigenous: native.

joint-stock company: a company made up of people who pool their fortunes together. In the 1600s, investors formed a joint-stock company called the Virginia Company to gain profit from colonizing the New World.

malnutrition: not getting enough essential food elements such as vitamins and minerals to keep one's body healthy.

mica: a colored or transparent mineral that can be split into sheets.

mutiny: to revolt against one's superior officer, specifically on a ship.

pardon: to forgive anything illegal that a person has done.

pitch: a dark, sticky substance used for waterproofing and paving.

plantation: a large farm where one crop is grown.

pneumonia: a disease of the lungs that includes coughing, fever, chest pain, and chills.

Protestant: a Christian who does not belong to the Catholic Church.

sawyer: a person who earns his or her living by sawing wood.

shackle: a metal band fastened around the ankle or wrist. Shackles are usually chained to the floor or wall. They prevent a person from moving.

smallpox: a disease that causes a blister-like skin rash, vomiting, fever, and fatigue. The blisters become scars.

statehouse: the building where a community's legislature meets.

stockade: a line of posts that forms a walled enclosure. Stockades can be used to pen people in or as a defense to keep enemies out.

tuberculosis: a bacterial infection of oxygen-rich areas of the body such as the lungs.

typhus: a bacterial disease spread by lice that causes fever and a dark red rash.

veto: the right of one member of a decision-making group to stop an action by the group.

INDEX